THE WORLD'S MOST

World's Most Freaky Animals

Elizabeth Ginis

Please visit our website, www.garethstevens.com. For a free color catalog of all our high-quality books, call toll free 1-800-542-2595 or fax 1-877-542-2596.

Cataloging-in-Publication Data

Names: Ginis, Elizabeth.
Title: World's most freaky animals / Elizabeth Ginis.
Description: New York : Gareth Stevens, 2022. | Series: The world's most | Includes glossary and index.
Identifiers: ISBN 9781538274712 (pbk.) | ISBN 9781538274736 (library bound) | ISBN 9781538274729 (6 pack) | ISBN 9781538274743 (ebook)
Subjects: LCSH: Animals–Juvenile literature. | Animals–Miscellanea–Juvenile literature.
Classification: LCC QL49.M385 2022 | DDC 590–dc23

World's Most Freaky: © 2016 by Australian Geographic,
an imprint of Australian Geographic Holdings Ply Ltd.

Published in 2022 by
Gareth Stevens Publishing
29 E. 21st Street
New York, NY 10010

Editor: Lauren Smith
Book design: Katherine McKinnon

All rights reserved. No part of this book may be reproduced in any form without permission in writing from the publisher, except by a reviewer.

Printed in the United States of America

CPSIA compliance information: Batch #CWGS22: For further information contact Gareth Stevens, New York, New York at 1-800-542-2595.

PHOTOGRAPHER AND ILLUSTRATOR CREDITS
Listed by page, clockwise from top left.

Front Cover: Don Mnammoser/Shutterstock (SS), CamaleonFarm/Getty, Dave Fleetham/Getty, Maslov Dmity/SS, Eric Isselee/SS, Tomas Kotouc/SS; Back Cover: a_v_d/SS, Johan Larson/SS, Jeff Rotman/Getty, New Saetiew/SS, Dr Morley Read/SS, Reptiles4all/SS, Paravyan Eduard/SS, Ondrej Prosicky/SS; Page 1: Fabio Maffei/SS; Page 4: Nokuro/SS, Auscape/Getty, Blue Orange Studio/SS; Page 5: Nick Hobgood/Wikimedia, Andaman/SS, China Foto Press/Getty, Colette3/SS; Page 6: Nachalati/SS, Kate Capture/SS, Orlandin/SS, Borut Furlan/Getty; Page 7: Auscape/Getty, Auscape/Getty, Stephen Dalton/Getty; Page 8: Lee Yiu Tung/SS, THPStock/SS; Page 9: Brandelet/SS, Marion Kraschl/SS, Wildlife Reservation/SS, Rittmeyer et al/PLcS ONE; Page 10: Philippe Psaila/SPL/Getty, IvanaOK/Getty; Page 11: Joe McDonald/SS, Jelger Herder/ Buiten-beeld/Getty, Wil Meinderts/Buiten-beeld/Getty, Martin Pelanek/SS, BMJ/SS; Page 12: Volodymyr Burdiak/SS, Martin P/SS, Oxford Scientific/Getty, Stephen Dalton/Getty, Andrey Nekrasov/Getty; Page 13: Rui Manuel Teles Gomes/SS, Alexandr Junek Imaging s.r.o./SS, ArCaLu/SS; Page 14: Shulevskyy Volodymyr/SS, Reptiles4all/SS; Page 15: Buena Vista Images/Getty, Tambako the Jaguar/Getty, Ecoprint/SS, Johan Swanepoel/SS; Page 16: David Haring/DUPC/Getty, Ryan M Bolton/SS; Page 17: Reptiles4all/SS, Mint Images/Frans Lanting/Getty, Andrej Kubik/SS, Eduard Kyslynskyy/SS; Page 18: Tony Wear/SS; Page 19: Marilyn Connell/Tiaro Landcare, Gavriel Jecan/Getty, Stephan M. Höhne/Wikimedia, Bill Hatcher/Australian Geographic; Page 20: Dave Fleetham/Getty, Andrea Izzotti/SS, Belizar/SS; Page 21: Matt Chan/Flickr, Kevein Stead/Australian Geographic, SeraphP/SS, Katarina Christenson/SS, Katarina Christenson/SS; Page 22: Gregory A. Pozhvanov/SS; Page 23: Eric Isselee/SS, Aecole2010/Flickr, Brian Lasenby/SS; Page 24: Mavourneen/SS, A Lein/SS, Ultrashock/SS, Nicholas Smythe/Getty; Page 25: Dave Fleetham/Design Pics/Getty, Rusty Dodson/SS, Visuals Unlimited, Inc./Ken Catania/Getty; Page 26: Martin Mecnarowski/SS, Mark Caunt/SS; Page 27: Visuals Unlimited, Inc./Andres Morya/Getty, Nicholas Smythe/Getty, Vilainecrevette/SS; Page 28: Roland Seitre/Getty, Rosa Jay/SS, Thatje et al/PLoS One, Barcroft Media/Getty; Page 29: Dirk Ercken/SS, Dr. Morley Read/SS; Page 30: Elkin Restrepo/SS, Martin Mecnarowski/SS; Page 31: Christine Schmidt/Flickr, John Cancalosi/Getty, Rose Jay/SS; Page 32: Ryan M. Bolton/SS; Ends: Vasmila/SS

CONTENTS

ASIA 4
EUROPE 10
AFRICA 14
OCEANIA 18
NORTH AMERICA 22
SOUTH AMERICA 26
GLOSSARY 32
INDEX 32
FOR MORE INFORMATION 32

ASIA

PROBOSCIS MONKEY

No other primate has such a large, fleshy, dangling nose as the male proboscis monkey. It's believed the nose helps increase the volume of their call, impressing females and intimidating rivals. Proboscis monkeys have evolved webbed feet and hands to swim quickly, a great help when evading the crocodiles that lurk in the rivers of their native Borneo. Proboscis monkeys can't eat ripe fruit, as the sugar ferments and expands in their bellies, causing them to bloat, which can be deadly. They eat unripe fruit, as well as leaves and seeds. Habitat destruction throughout Borneo means this big-nosed primate is endangered.

FACT BOX — JUMPING IN

Enthusiastic swimmers, both males and females are often seen launching themselves from trees to belly flop into the water below.

COCONUT OCTOPUS

The only **invertebrate** known to use tools, and one of only two octopuses known to "walk" on two of its legs, the coconut octopus is named for its habit of carrying coconut shells across the seafloor and using them to build fortresses. Before construction can begin, the octopus must dig up and thoroughly clean its building materials. During this time the shells afford no protection, leaving the **cephalopod** open to attack from predators including fish and crabs.

FACT BOX: CRAZY FOR COCONUTS
When threatened, the octopus retreats into the two halves of its coconut shell and pulls them together, forming a near **impenetrable** orb.

TUFTED DEER

By far the scariest-looking deer on the planet, this vampiric deer has oversized, protruding canine teeth that look like fangs. Males use their short tusks during mating season (September to December) to fend off rivals. When threatened or startled, they also bark loudly. Named for the distinctive patch of coarse hair on its forehead, which often hides its small antlers, the tufted deer lives in high-altitude forest regions in north-eastern Myanmar (formerly known as Burma) and southern and central China.

RUN RABBIT RUN
If disturbed, the tufted deer takes flight. Moving with rabbit-like jumps and flashing the white underside of its tail, it confuses predators just long enough to escape.

EMEI MOUSTACHE TOAD

Mating season for the Emei moustache toad is a macho affair. In February and March each year, males sprout 10 to 16 spines on their top lip and migrate from the forest to swift-flowing rivers to breed. They compete for territory and females by head-butting each other's bellies, often causing puncture wounds. When mating is done and the eggs have spawned, the spines fall out and the fighters return to the forest.

FACT BOX: MAN UP
In the frog world, male frogs that grow larger than their female counterparts (as is the case with the Emei moustache toad) are known to be aggressive. In up to 90 percent of frog species, females are larger.

5

ASIA

WREATHED HORNBILL

This distinctive bird has specialized ridges on the top of its beak. Called casques, they signify dominance and gender. Mating for life, the wreathed hornbill has a breeding practice akin to an ancient Egyptian burial: When the female is ready to lay her eggs, she builds a nest in a tree cavity. The male then entombs her in the cavity, sealing it with mud, fruit, and feces and leaving only a slender hole through which he feeds her and their chicks. For roughly four months, the female and her offspring depend solely on the male for their survival.

FACT BOX: COLOR CODE

The gender of wreathed hornbills is easily distinguished by the color of their throats. The male's throat is yellow and the female's is blue.

MIMIC OCTOPUS

Using color matching and shape-shifting, this clever cephalopod avoids the jaws of its predators. It imitates a range of creatures, including a poisonous flatfish scooting along the seafloor and a lionfish swimming with its toxic spines erect. Maybe its most incredible morph, however, is when imitating the venomous banded sea snake: It conceals six of its arms in the sand and raises the other two, now colored with thick black and beige stripes, in opposite directions to resemble the reptile.

FACT BOX: MARINE MIMICRY

A jawfish in Indonesian oceans has trumped the expert mimic octopus—it mimics the mimic octopus! The yellow-and-black striped fish, which normally stays hidden, hitches a ride on the octopus, wiggling its body like an extra tentacle.

FLYING DRAGON

FAST FACT

While some other lizards also have small patagia, or flaps of skin along their ribs, members of the flying dragon genus (*Draco*) are the only known reptiles recognized as "true" gliders.

Soaring on outstretched wings, the flying dragon lizard moves effortlessly around its native forests in Southeast Asia and India. The wings are actually skin extensions called patagia. They allow the lizard to easily glide through the air. The maximum flight **trajectory** for both males and females is 26 feet (8 m), or 40 times its body length. Their patagia also help identify different species, as each of the 45 known species of flying dragon lizards has a unique color display.

7

ASIA

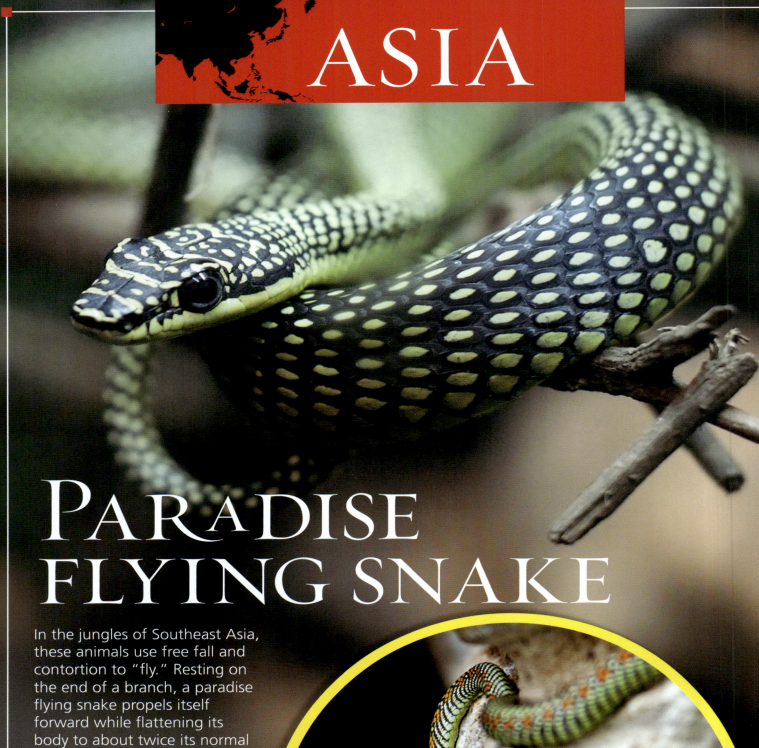

Paradise flying snake

In the jungles of Southeast Asia, these animals use free fall and contortion to "fly." Resting on the end of a branch, a paradise flying snake propels itself forward while flattening its body to about twice its normal width, giving it a downward C shape, which traps air. To turn, it wriggles back and forth. The paradise tree snake, which can have green, yellow, or orange spots, is one of the smaller flying snakes, measuring about 2 feet (60 cm) in length, and the best glider. It's been recorded traveling up to 328 feet (100 m) through the air.

FACT BOX — HIGH FLYERS

All five species of flying snakes are better gliders than their mammalian equivalents, gliding possums. They range from 2 to 4 feet (0.6 to 1.2 m) in length and eat bats, birds, frogs, lizards, and rats. While mildly venomous, their tiny fangs won't hurt humans.

HAMMERHEAD SHARK

It's obvious how this shark got its name! Its wide-set eyes and mallet-shaped head are used to find and attack fish, nailing them to the seafloor. Covering its expansive snout are thousands of sensory organs called the ampullae of Lorenzini. They're used to detect the electrical fields created by prey animals. This is useful for hunting down its favorite meal, stingrays, which usually bury themselves under the sand. There are nine species of hammerhead shark, but only one, the great hammerhead, is considered dangerous to people.

FACT BOX: BURIED TREASURE

Swimming above the ocean floor, hammerheads swing their T-shaped heads from side to side, like you would a metal detector on a beach, looking for prey.

PAEDOPHRYNE AMAUENSIS

At just 0.2 inch (7 mm) long, and the size of a fly, *Paedophryne amauensis* is the world's smallest **vertebrate**. Found in the eastern rain forests of Papua New Guinea, it lives in leaf litter on the forest floor and eats tiny invertebrates, such as mites, which are ignored by bigger predators. They're adept jumpers and they can leap 30 times the length of their body. Their high-pitched call sounds like that of an insect and is difficult for humans to hear, which is perhaps why it went undiscovered until 2009.

HOPPING ON

Unlike other frogs, *Paedophryne amauensis's* life cycle doesn't include a tadpole phase. They hatch as "hoppers," or miniature versions of the adults.

LESSER MOUSE DEER

The smallest known hoofed mammal, the lesser mouse deer grows to about 18 inches (45 cm) and weighs a mere 4 pounds (2 kg). It appears to be a mix of deer and mouse, but it's neither. It's a member of the *Tragulidae* family, which literally means "tiny goat." Normally docile, males will angrily beat their hooves when alarmed, stomping on the ground up to seven times per second. This drumroll usually scares away predators, but if forced to fight, it will use its tusklike canine teeth to tear at its foe.

QUICK ESCAPE

With a body the size of a rabbit's and short legs as thin as pencils, the lesser mouse deer is just the right size to scamper through the tangled undergrowth of the tropical forests of Southeast Asia.

EUROPE

FACT BOX: CAVE DRAGON

Native to central and southeastern Europe, the olm is listed as vulnerable. Your best chance of seeing it is in Slovenia's Postojna Cave, where underwater cameras and TV monitors show its secretive aquatic antics. Centuries ago, when floods washed them from their caves, people believed they were baby dragons!

OLM

There's nothing normal about this slippery salamander: It's blind, only found in underground rivers, swims like an eel, able to go 10 years without eating, and lives to 100. The olm spends its whole life underwater, and finds food using sensitive sensors in its snout. Females lay eggs only once or twice in their lifetime, on the ceiling of a cave, and can smell if the young inside is growing or not. If not, she eats it!

WALRUS

Tusks, moustache-like whiskers, wrinkled pinky-brown skin, and a blubber-filled body combine to make this marine mammal unique. It uses its tusks to pull itself out of the water, earning it the name "tooth-walker," and also to break breathing holes in the Arctic ice from underneath. The tusks can grow up to 3.2 feet (1 m) long, and males also use them in fights over territory and females.

FAST FACT

A walrus's whiskers are called vibrissae and help it feel for food, especially shellfish, on the dark ocean floor.

RUFF

It's the ring of puffed-up neck feathers that give this bird its name: a ruff was an ornamental collar worn by people living in Europe during the mid-16th to 17th centuries. Only breeding males display the ruff. It also has a tuft of brightly colored feathers on top of its head, and orange legs, beak, and rough facial skin. Once mating is finished, the fancy feathers **molt** and the face, beak, and legs become duller. **Endemic** to Europe, this migratory bird has been found as far afield as Australia.

READY TO FIGHT

Known for its aggressive displays at communal mating grounds, called leks, ruffs also go by the scientific name of *Philomachus pugnus*, which translates to "battle loving."

EUROPEAN RIVER LAMPREY

Like something from a vampire movie, this jawless eel-like species attaches itself to larger fish and drinks their blood. Its round, sucker-like mouth contains two rows of circular teeth that help it cling to its host as it swims. It has one nostril and seven small breathing holes along each side of its body behind the eyes.

SPAWN AND DIE

Similar to salmon, European river lamprey migrate from coastal waters to inland breeding grounds to **spawn**. They swim upstream in autumn and winter, lay eggs in the spring, and die. Their young take a few years to mature, feeding on bacteria in the stream before heading out to sea.

EUROPE

EUROPEAN BADGER

Like bears, European badgers **hibernate** in the winter, settling into burrows to wait out the big chill. They put on large amounts of body fat during the summer, which nourishes them throughout the cold, dark months underground. Up to 12 animals might cram into a den, which has a series of tunnels running off it to above ground openings. With a head of black, white, and silver fur, this kindly creature is a lover not a fighter, sharing its burrow with other animals, including rabbits, red foxes, and raccoon dogs.

BOOKS OF BADGERS

European folklore and fairy tales are filled with badgers, although they're usually not friendly! In *The Wind in the Willows*, Mr. Badger is a grumpy fellow who "simply hates society." An evil badger called Tommy Brock kidnaps children in Beatrix Potter's *The Tale of Mr. Tod*.

SHORT-SNOUTED SEAHORSE

With the head of a horse, a long, forward-curling tail, and a set of spiny eyelashes, this seahorse is an unlikely looking creature. The short-snouted seahorse measures just 5 inches (13 cm) from head to tail, and is able to change color, from green and yellow to maroon, purple, and black, to mimic the plants in which it lives. These little beauties are found in shallow coastal waters off the United Kingdom, Western Europe, and the Mediterranean.

FACT BOX — PUSHY BEHAVIOR

Males are aggressive when fighting for a mate: they use their snouts to shove their rivals and their tails to wrestle one another. Males and females mate for life, and males carry the eggs in a **brood** pouch on their stomach.

DIVING BELL SPIDER

This clever little arachnid only needs to come to the surface of its pond once a day to breathe: It spins a web underwater and fills it with oxygen. Using the fine hairs on its abdomen, it moves tiny bubbles of air from above the water surface to its underwater "diving bell." The bubble works a bit like a fish's gills, taking oxygen from the water and sending carbon dioxide back out.

WHAT A DIVE

Diving bell spiders live in still waterways throughout Europe and are the only spider species that lives their entire lives underwater, mating, laying eggs, and catching prey from their webs.

OCEAN SUNFISH

One of the ocean's true oddities, this disc-shaped creature is the world's largest bony fish, measuring up to 11 feet (3.3 m) in diameter and weighing in at an astounding 4,960 pounds (2,250 kg). Its bullet shape is the result of a tail fin that never grows. It folds in on itself, instead, and forms a rudder called a clavus. Often seen sunbathing near the ocean's surface, its oversized dorsal fin cuts through the water and is commonly mistaken for a shark's. But don't fear; this giant fish only has a taste for jellyfish, algae, and **zooplankton.**

FACT BOX: PESKY PARASITES
Sunfish become so overrun with parasites, they jump up to 10 feet (3 m) out of the ocean, landing with a slap, to try to get rid of them.

GREATER FLAMINGO

This regal-looking bird owes its exquisite pink color to the animals it eats, which are shrimplike crustaceans that live in the saltwater mudflats of southwestern Europe. Stirring up the mud with its webbed feet, the flamingo buries its long, bent beak, and sometimes its whole head, in the water to suck up the tiny treats. Its tongue pumps up and down, pushing the water out of its mouth and trapping the food in tiny filters. The greater flamingo is the largest of the family at 5 feet (1.5 m) tall.

FAST FACT
Greater flamingos live and breed in colonies of up to 200,000. There's safety in numbers: While some birds stand watch, others can feed. A loud, deep warning honk, similar to that of a goose, alerts them to predators.

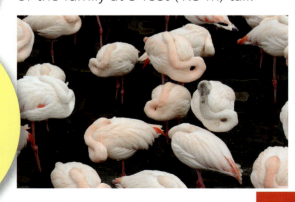

13

AFRICA

JACKSON'S CHAMELEON

Looking like a mini triceratops, the Jackson's chameleon has three spiky horns protruding from its face. It's because of this amazing headgear that it's also called the three-horned chameleon. Found in the mountains of Kenya and Tanzania, it lives in trees and mimics its surroundings, changing its skin color to match the twigs and foliage, and rocking back and forth in time with the rustling leaves. Only males have horns; they use them to defend territory. Locking them together, they try to push each other off the branch.

FAST FACT

Born brown, Jackson's chameleon babies turn bright green four months later! They grow to about the length of a ruler, about 1 foot (30 cm).

HIPPOPOTAMUS

This short, stocky, water-loving mammal is all kinds of odd. Its name is derived from the Greek word for "river horse," but its closest living relatives are pigs, whales, and dolphins. Like the latter, a hippopotamus needs to stay moist—so much so that its skin releases an oily, red fluid first thought to be blood but now believed to be a sunscreen, moisturizer, and antibiotic. Hippos can stay underwater for five minutes before coming up for air. Even when they're sleeping, their bodies automatically bob to the surface so they can take a breath, then they sink back to the bottom.

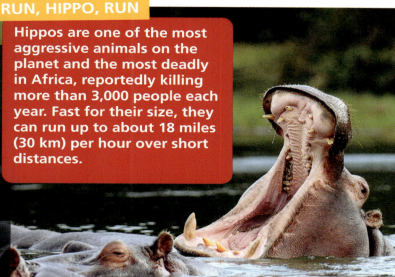

RUN, HIPPO, RUN
Hippos are one of the most aggressive animals on the planet and the most deadly in Africa, reportedly killing more than 3,000 people each year. Fast for their size, they can run up to about 18 miles (30 km) per hour over short distances.

SOCIAL WEAVERS

Common in the Kalahari region of southern Africa, these finch-sized birds build the largest tree nests in the world, measuring up to 20 feet (6 m) wide by 10 feet (3 m) tall. This extraordinary nest may house up to 100 families at any one time. Some nests are used for more than 100 years! From a distance you could mistake them for haystacks hanging in a tree. Sometimes, nests become so heavy they topple the tree from which they hang.

THIRSTY MUCH?
Sociable weavers drink less water than any other bird and most never take a sip. They get all their moisture from their food: bugs.

HONEY BADGER

Strong, smart, and fierce, honey badgers, or ratels, have a thick, coarse, black-and-white coat that might remind you of a skunk. It's not just their appearance that's similar; when threatened, a honey badger releases a "stink bomb" that repels predators like lions, leopards, and hyenas. If that doesn't work, the honey badger's skin is really thick, which means it's hard to pierce, and loose, so it can turn around in it and bite its attacker.

FACT BOX — WHAT'S YOUR POISON?
Honey badgers have a strong **immunity** to the venom of snakes and scorpions, which is useful because they're the badger's favorite meals!

AFRICA

AYE-AYE

With its transfixed stare and wild fur, the critically endangered aye-aye has long been considered an omen of bad luck by the people of its native Madagascar. Related to chimpanzees, apes, and humans, these primates use their sharp claws and opposable big toes to dangle from branches in rain forest trees. While perched there, the aye-aye raps its long middle finger on the bark and listens for wriggling insect larvae in the wood. It fishes them out with the same pointed claw, which is also used for scooping the flesh out of coconuts. The aye-aye is the only primate known to use echolocation (calling out and listening for an echo) to find dinner.

SATANIC LEAF-TAILED GECKO

With its demonic red eyes, angular horns, and wicked smile, it's an easy guess as to how the satanic leaf-tailed gecko got its name. Native to the rain forests of Madagascar, it also has an alarming, bright red mouth that it uses to warn off predators. If you don't scare easily, then consider the gecko's other defense mechanism: camouflage. It'd be easy to think you were picking up a fallen leaf instead of the tail of this tiny gecko. And even if you did, it would likely drop its tail and scamper away.

FACT BOX — LEAF ME ALONE

The satanic leaf-tailed gecko doesn't just look like a leaf, it acts like one too, spending most of the day hanging motionless off a branch or curled among leaf litter.

ARMADILLO LIZARD

Measuring just 8 inches (20 cm) long and covered in spiny scales, the armadillo lizard rolls into a ball, tail in mouth, underbelly protected, when threatened. Native to the west coast of South Africa, this fierce-looking lizard has such a powerful bite that it's been known to break its own jaw while eating. It lives in large family groups and eats bugs and spiders.

FAST FACT

The armadillo lizard's head, body, and tail are all flattened, allowing it to squeeze into rock crevices for protection from predators such as eagles, snakes, and mongooses.

GERENUK

This giraffe-necked gazelle has muscular hind legs that allow it to stand upright. By using its front legs to bend branches downward, it can nibble leaves high off the ground. It also has oversized rabbitlike ears, which are always listening for approaching predators as well as other gerenuks. The antelope uses several sounds to communicate: a buzzing when alarmed, a whistle when annoyed, and a loud bleat when in extreme danger.

GIRAFFE

No other land animal on Earth is as tall as the giraffe. If you were on the second floor of a building, a giraffe could easily gaze in on you through the window. Its neck is as long as its legs, about 6 feet (1.8 m), and its feet are the diameter of a dinner plate. In fact, everything about the giraffe is oversized: Its tongue stretches up to 1.5 feet (0.5 m). That long tongue is black, which protects it from the scorching African sun.

NAKED MOLE RAT

Looking like a cross between an uncooked sausage and a miniature walrus, the naked mole rat fits in a teacup. These virtually hairless mammals live in colonies of 20 to 300 individuals in an area around the same size as six football fields, and rarely leave the safety of their sandy burrows in sub-Saharan Africa. Like bees and ants, the colony is led by a queen. Foot soldiers dig the burrows, collect food, and tend the young, but she's the only one allowed to breed.

OH DEER!
A gerenuk can go its whole life without drinking water, getting all the moisture it needs from its herbivorous diet of shoots, leaves, herbs, flowers, and fruit.

COAT OF ARMS
The pattern of a giraffe's coat is unique, just like a human fingerprint. The shape of the patterning reflects where they live in Africa.

YOU EAT WHAT?
Naked mole rats eat roots and bulbs, but have also been known to eat their own poop, collecting extra nutrients, and even chew through concrete.

OCEANIA

Leafy Sea Dragon

Dripping with "leaves," this sea dragon blends perfectly with the seaweed and kelp forests off southern Australia where it lives. Closely related to seahorses, it drifts with the currents in search of microscopic prey, like sea lice. With a thin, tubular snout and small leaf-shaped fins, it's usually brown-yellow in color and about 14 inches (35 cm) from top to tail.

FAST FACT

A bright yellow tail on a male leafy sea dragon is a sign he's ready to mate. Like seahorses, males are in charge of childbearing. Unlike seahorses, which carry their young in a pouch on the stomach, male sea dragons nurture theirs on the underside of the tail.

MARY RIVER TURTLE

At about 20 inches (50 cm) in length, the endangered Mary River turtle is one of Australia's largest. But it's not its size that's most interesting. It's the fact that it uses its enormously long tail to breathe. This unusual feature means the turtle breathes through its butt! It also has exceptionally long, whisker-like "barbels" on its chin. Inside them are its taste buds. They help it feel out food.

BOTTOMS UP
In turtles, as with reptiles, the back passage is called a cloaca. Urine and feces, as well as eggs, pass out through here.

TREE KANGAROO
Unlike their ground-dwelling cousins, tree kangaroos have long, muscular arms and short legs. They also have curved nails and spongy pads that help with gripping, while a long tail helps with balance. Graceful climbers, they wrap their arms around tree trunks and hop upward using their hind legs. They are expert jumpers too, leaping from tree to tree and down to the ground.

GIANT PRICKLY STICK INSECT
Covered in thorns, the female giant prickly stick insect is intimidating. At almost 8 inches (20 cm) long, she's twice as big as a male, and sprays an odor to scare off predators. While males do this too, they're more likely to fly away from danger. However, a female's wings are too small, and her body too heavy, for flight.

SUPERB BIRD OF PARADISE
When an adult male superb bird of paradise wants to attract a female, he fans out the velvety black feathers on his back and the gleaming blue feathers on his chest to form a cape. He then begins snapping his tail feathers and hopping around in a fancy dance, hoping a female will mate with him. At just 10 inches (26 cm) long, he's the world's smallest superhero!

NO SWEAT
The 17 species live in the steamy rain forests of New Guinea and northeastern Australia, keeping cool by licking their arms and letting the moisture evaporate.

HOME AMONG THE GUM TREES
These insects live in eucalyptus forests in northeastern Australia and can be found in a variety of earthy colors, which helps them blend in to the trees.

HEAVENLY CREATURES
These stunning birds live in the forests of New Guinea. The local name for them means "birds of the gods."

19

OCEANIA

GUINEAFOWL PUFFERFISH

With its torpedo-shaped body, big head, and large eyes, this fish is best known for its talent for inflating like a balloon to scare off predators. To do this, it drinks lots of water to fill its extremely elastic stomach. But this isn't its only defense: It's also covered in spines and is highly poisonous if eaten. The guineafowl pufferfish can be either bright yellow or black with yellow spots. The dark ones are more toxic.

FAST FACT

It has four large, constantly growing teeth that are joined together to form a beak-like structure. It eats squid, krill, clams, crabs, and other hard-shelled crustaceans to help wear them down.

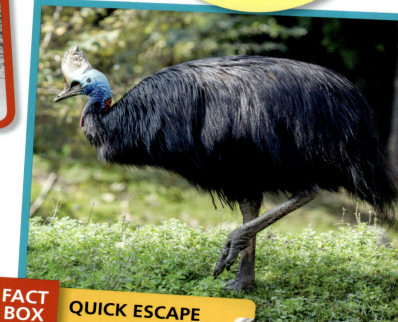

CASSOWARY

Standing as tall as a person, Australia's most dangerous bird has a stretched neck, a scaly blue head, and wattles, or red flaps of skin that hang from its throat. But it's what sits atop its head that's most eye-catching: a helmet made of toughened skin, hard on the outside but spongy inside. Males raise the young, and will protect them at any cost. A cassowary's long middle claw is like a dagger and can be used to disembowel some predators.

FACT BOX: QUICK ESCAPE

A shy creature, the cassowary is elusive quarry. People can search for years and never spot one, or catch a glimpse as it high-tails it into the rain forests of northeastern Australia.

PLATYPUS

When first discovered by Europeans, this old-looking mammal was described as a cross between a duck and a beaver. Today, we know it as unique to Australia and one of only two egg-laying mammals, the other being the echidna. It has a large rubbery bill, streamlined body, and flat club-like tail that stores fat. The claws on its front feet are used for digging burrows in riverbanks, while its webbed legs and feet make it an adept swimmer.

FACT BOX — KILLER SPURS

The platypus is one of the world's few venomous mammals. Males have a sharp spur on their ankles, which is connected to a venom gland in the upper leg. While the venom won't kill you, the pain it causes is reported to be excruciating.

CUTTLEFISH

This oceanic master of disguise changes color depending on its surroundings. It has eight arms, two tentacles, three hearts, and one of the largest brains, compared to its body size, of all invertebrates. It's also not a fish, but a **mollusk**, and has a sharp, beak-like mouth that it uses like scissors to cut open flesh. It then uses its tentacles to tear out the meat.

WRAPAROUND SPIDER

Colored to conceal and happily overlooked, this spider is perfectly built for tree hugging. Its body is shaped like a shield: The underside is concave to fit snugly around a branch, and its abdomen is slightly raised to complete the line. Some even have bumps or turrets on their back so they look just like a tiny twig.

SPLAT SPIDER

Ideally disguised by day, this Australian native builds large, orb-shaped webs between trees at night to catch its insect prey.

FACT BOX — POLLY WANT A CUTTLEBONE

White, feather-shaped cuttlebone washes up on the beach. It's unique to cuttlefish and what keeps it afloat. While jewelers use it to make molds for small objects, it's often given to pet birds as a source of calcium.

21

NORTH AMERICA

GLASSWING BUTTERFLY

While most butterflies have colorful, patterned wings, designed to warn off predators, this species uses invisibility as its defensive cloak. Its wings are all but transparent. But that's not all that's amazing: this butterfly's 2.3-inch-wide (6 cm) wings can carry roughly 40 times its own weight. It's also exceptionally fast, flying at speeds of up to 8 miles (13 km) per hour.

FAST FACT

The glasswing butterfly's Spanish name is *espejitos*, which means "little mirrors."

AXOLOTL

Also known as Mexican walking fish, axolotls are not fish at all but amphibians. Like frogs and toads, they breathe through their gills, three on each side of the head just above the legs, and skin. But unlike other amphibians, they don't develop past the larval stage (that's the tadpole phase in frogs). If they did, they would become salamanders. Native to Mexico, axolotls are considered critically endangered.

HEALING POWER

An axolotl can heal almost any injured part of its body, regenerating arms, legs, tail, skin, and even major organs such as the heart, liver, and kidney.

NORTH AMERICAN BEAVER

The first thing you'll notice about a beaver is its teeth. Large and strong, they're used to gnaw down trees and build dome-shaped homes, called lodges. Powerful webbed back feet and a paddle-shaped tail help beavers swim at up to 5 miles (8 km) per hour. They can stay underwater for 15 minutes at a time.

FACT BOX — LEAVE IT TO BEAVER

Beavers are second only to humans in their ability to change their environment, felling trees to transform forests and fields into ponds.

FLANNEL MOTH CATERPILLAR

Despite its furry coat, petting this creature is definitely a no-no. The hairy comb-over conceals small, exceptionally poisonous spines that stick in the skin and cause excruciating pain that lingers for up to 12 hours. If you do happen to pet a flannel moth caterpillar, the best way to remove the spines is with sticky tape. Lay it over the site and rip it off. This caterpillar morphs into a flannel moth, which also has a pretty hairdo, but is harmless.

CAN'T TOUCH THIS

Another of the caterpillar's charming traits is its method of poop removal: It flings its feces away from its body to prevent parasites from being attracted to it.

NORTH AMERICA

BURROWING OWL

These ground-dwelling owls nest in burrows dug by other animals, including squirrels, armadillos, skunks, or gophers, in the open plains throughout North America. Galloping across the ground on their long legs, they pounce on prey, including insects, small mammals, amphibians, reptiles, and other birds, around dawn and dusk. Left on their own in the burrow while the parents hunt, juvenile owlets scare off predators by mimicking the sounds of a rattlesnake.

FAST FACT
Burrowing owls surround their nests with mammal waste. The stinky concoction attracts dung beetles, one of the owl's favorite foods.

SOLENODON

The elongated snout of the solenodon is unusually flexible. This means it can twist and turn its snout to probe tiny nooks and crannies for food. Native to the islands of Cuba and Hispaniola, the endangered solenodon is one of very few venomous mammals. Similar to a snake, it injects its poison through teeth that have special grooves to carry the venom.

FACT BOX — GRUNT WORK
The female solenodon has two nipples for feeding her young at the rear end of her stomach. When threatened, solenodons grunt like pigs and also make birdlike cries.

NORTH AMERICAN PORCUPINE

This prickly character wears a coat of quills: a pointed warning that it's not easy prey. Its needlelike spines lie flat until it's threatened, and then bristle on command. The North American porcupine is the largest member of its species, reaching over 3 feet (1 m) in length, and has more than 30,000 barbed quills. Each one has a sharp tip, and is difficult to remove once stuck in a predator's skin.

TO THE POINT
Great climbers, porcupines spend much of their time in trees. They use their large front teeth to devour wood, bark, and stems, and will even chow down on canoe paddles.

24

NARWHAL

These unicorns of the sea have a swordlike spiral protruding from their heads. The ivory tusk is actually a really long tooth, and grows much longer in males, up to half their body length. Scientists believe the tusk is used in mating rituals to impress females or fight rivals. Related to bottlenose dolphins, beluga whales, and orcas, narwhals travel in pods of up to 20, but have been seen in groups of several thousand in the Arctic waters off Canada, Greenland, Norway, and Russia.

NORSE NAME
"Narwhal" comes from the old Norse word *nar*, meaning "corpse." The mammals were so named because they resembled the bodies of drowned sailors.

STAR-NOSED MOLE

Resembling a blend of rat and octopus, the star-nosed mole uses its unique snout to find food. The 22 tentacles, which together have a diameter of 0.4 inch (1 cm), ring the nostrils and work as a tactile eye, feeling for prey. They work so quickly that they've earned the mole the award of fastest-eating mammal, taking around one-tenth of a second to identify and eat a piece of food. This nose also lets the mole smell underwater. The mole blows bubbles, which mingle with the scent of a small fish or earthworm, then sucks them back in—and then it's mealtime!

FACT BOX — HAIRY HANDFUL
With its large, scaled feet and long, thick tail, the star-nosed mole fits comfortably on an adult hand. It lives in the wetlands of eastern Canada and the northeastern United States.

TEXAS HORNED LIZARD

Wearing a crown of thorns, the tiny Texas horned lizard also goes by the name horny toad because of its rounded body, which it puffs up when threatened. Its other defense mechanism is to shoot a stream of blood from the corners of its eyes and occasionally its mouth. The liquid, which can travel up to 15 times the length of the lizard's body, is a cocktail of blood and chemicals that's foul-tasting to predators such as wolves and coyotes.

GAME OF THORNS
The lizard's horns are bony extensions of its skull and are part of its armor, along with its spiked scales.

25

SOUTH AMERICA

POTOO

Sitting motionless on the stump of a branch, matching its color, and with beak pointed skyward, this bird is easy to miss during daylight hours. At night, its huge staring eyes and eerie call, "po-TOO, po-TOO," light up the South American forests where it lives. Swooping from its perch, it hunts for flying insects and swallows them whole thanks to its large, wide mouth.

FACT BOX — LUCKY SONG

Of the seven species, the largest is the great potoo. It has a wingspan of 3.2 feet (1 m) and makes a unique moaning growl that's unsettlingly eerie when heard in the jungle at night. According to Brazilian legend, it's a song from the dead, giving good luck to friends and bad luck to enemies.

COMMON BASILISK

This amazing animal runs on water. When threatened, it escapes by sprinting to the water's edge and keeps going. The reptile runs on its back legs, body upright and arms by its side. It's so good on water because its big feet have flaps of scaly skin along the toes that create air bubbles, which it then pushes down on to keep it afloat. As long as it moves quickly, it won't sink. And fast it is: It's been clocked at more than 5 miles (8 km) per hour on water and even swifter on land, speeding along at almost 7 miles (11 km) per hour.

FACT BOX — SINK OR SWIM

Juveniles can run atop water for up to 65 feet (20 m), while adults make it only a quarter of that distance. It's not because they're slower, they just weigh more. Don't worry about them drowning though, they're great swimmers and can also stay underwater for more than half an hour. That's plenty of time to escape even the most patient predator.

BROWN-THROATED SLOTH

There's a lot that's unusual about this mammal. Its thick, brown fur regularly looks green-blue because of the algae growing on it. This coloring helps it stay well hidden in its rain forest home. Instead of toes, it has three long claws on its front and back feet that help it hang upside down from branches. It can swivel its head to almost 90 degrees, and its mouth is shaped in a permanent smile. The size of a cat, it weighs around 9 pounds (4 k) and rarely walks, staying in the trees except when it needs to poop, about once a week.

SLOW FOOD MOVEMENT

These herbivores eat leaves, twigs, and fruit. Because they move so little and use hardly any energy, a single meal can take up to one month to pass through the body.

PINK FAIRY ARMADILLO

While this little fairy doesn't have wings, it is definitely enchanting. At only 6 inches (15 cm) long, it's the smallest of all armadillos, has a fluffy white belly, and wears a coat of thin pink scales. The scales are so thin that they're almost translucent. It's the blood vessels underneath that give them their rosy glow. Living only on the sandy plains and arid grasslands of Argentina, it uses its oversized claws to dig burrows and find food, like ant larvae, worms, and other insects.

FACT BOX — PINK BITS

Little is known about this elusive species, but researchers believe its armor helps it thermoregulate (or keep its internal body temperature steady).

SOUTH AMERICA

KINKAJOU

Also known as honey bears because of their golden coat and appetite for sweet treats, kinkajous use their long, sticky tongues to raid bees' hives and termite nests. They live in the tropical rain forests of South America and have rotating ankles that let them run up and down tree trunks without having to turn their body. Their strong prehensile (gripping) tail is as long as their 20-inch (50 cm) body and acts like a third arm, allowing them to hang upside down from branches.

FACT BOX: SPREADING THE LOVE

Sometimes confused with monkeys, the kinkajou (pronounced KINK-a-joo) helps pollinate flowers. Pollen sticks to its face and then smears off at the next blossom it visits.

PANDA ANT

Don't be fooled by the cute appearance of this insect—it's actually a wasp whose sting packs a powerful punch. Found only in Chile, the panda ant is boldly colored to warn off predators. While males and females wear similar coats, they are often mistaken for different species. This is because the males are more than twice the size of females, have wings, and are nocturnal, unlike the females of the species.

FACT BOX: NESTING INSTINCT

Female panda ants lay their eggs in the nests of ground-living insects, such as bees and wasps. When they hatch, they eat the developing larvae of the original insect.

YETI CRAB

White, hairy, and rarely seen, yeti crabs flock to thermal vents in the floor of the icy Southern Ocean to keep warm. Thousands of the tiny crustaceans crawl over each other to get close to the boiling water without scalding themselves. There are three known species of yeti crab. The latest discovery, the Antarctic yeti crab, was found in 2010, and warms itself in waters up to 750°F (400°C).

MAKING DINNER

Because there's no sunlight where they live, these crabs farm their own food. The tiny hairs on their shell grow bacteria, which the crabs eat.

Yuruani Glass Frog

FAST FACT

Evergreen
The back of the Yuruani glass frog is yellowish-green with lime green blotches, which blends perfectly with the leaves on which it lives. It has bulging, golden-brown eyes.

Clearly, there are no secrets with this little amphibian: the skin covering its belly and chest cavity is transparent so you can see the internal organs, like the heart, and bones. Found on the leaves of shrubs and trees along streams, this delicate 1-inch (2 cm) frog also frequents waterways with brilliant red jasper rocks. Sticky pads and webbed toes allow it to lay its eggs on the underside of leaves that hang over the water. When hatched, the larvae fall into the stream below.

SOUTH AMERICA

Sword-Billed Hummingbird

The only species of bird to have a beak longer than its body, this sword-wielding hummingbird is perfectly designed to feed on flowers with tubular nectar chambers. Because its lance-like beak is so long, as is its tongue, it preens itself using its feet. From tail to beak tip it measures more than 9 inches (23 cm) and is one of the world's largest hummingbirds. While the sword-billed hummingbird feeds, its wings beat fast in 8-shaped movements while the tail is cocked. The hummingbird is very agile in the air and performs beautiful flight displays, especially during mating season.

FAST FACT

This unique bird sits with its beak angled upwards to balance it with its body weight. It's native to the Andes Mountains of the northwestern coast of South America.

ELECTRIC EEL

It's shocking, but this slippery snakelike creature isn't actually an eel. It's a knifefish, a freshwater species known for its ability to make electricity. The eel's long, cylindrical body contains cells, called electrocytes, that store power like microscopic batteries. When it's hunting or threatened, these cells release a charge of at least 600 volts—that's enough to shock a horse. Electric eels have flattened heads and are usually dark green or gray on top with a yellowish stomach. They live in streams of the Amazon and Orinoco basins in South America.

FACT BOX: DEADLY SHOCKING

Can the jolt from an electric eel kill a human? Not usually, but multiple shocks can stop the heart from beating. People have also drowned in shallow water after a shock.

BRAZILIAN PORCUPINE

With its oversized pinky-brown nose and soft, curious eyes, the Brazilian porcupine looks sweet enough to cuddle. But you wouldn't: It's covered in short, thick, white-yellow spines and has four long claws on each foot that can shred skin. The claws are designed to help with climbing. This animal spends more than three-quarters of its time in trees eating, sleeping, and socializing, and has a long tail that it uses to curl around branches.

TANTRUMS AND SPINES

Like a toddler, this little mammal stomps its feet and cries when scared or upset. If confronted by a predator, it pops its quills, making it look twice as big. And if that fails, it rolls up into a spiky ball.

SURINAM TOAD

Looking like a leaf or flat rock, this well-camouflaged toad has a unique way of caring for its young. The female carries her eggs under the skin on her back. The piggyback ride continues for three to four months. When fully formed, babies pop free and head for the water's surface to breathe. The mother then sheds her skin, ready for the next breeding season.

STAR-STUDDED

Also known as the star-fingered toad, this amphibian has a tiny star on the tip of each of the four fingers on its front legs. It lies with arms outstretched on the riverbed and uses them to feel for food. If something brushes against the stars, it sucks it up.

31

Glossary

brood — A family of offspring or young.
cephalopod — A class of mollusks that have tentacles attached to their heads.
endemic — Native to a particular country or locality.
hibernate — To spend the winter in a dormant condition.
immunity — Unable to be affected by a certain disease.
impenetrable — Unable to be pierced.
invertebrate — An animal without a backbone.
mollusk — A type of animal with a soft body and shell, including snails, bivalves, and squids.
molt — To cast or shed feathers.
spawn — The release of reproductive cells for fishes, amphibians, mollusks, and crustaceans.
trajectory — The curve of an object in flight.
vertebrate — An animal with a backbone.
zooplankton — Tiny animal organisms that float in the water.

Index

bird 6, 11, 13, 15, 19, 20, 24, 26, 30
breeding/mating 5, 6, 11, 12, 13, 17, 18, 19, 25, 30, 31
building 5, 6, 15, 21
eggs 6, 10, 11, 12, 19, 21, 28, 31
endangered 4, 16, 19, 23, 24

fish 6, 11, 13, 20, 31
mammal 8, 9, 11, 15, 17, 21, 24, 25
reptile 6, 7, 19, 27
spines 5, 23, 24, 31
tusks 5, 9, 11, 25
venom/poison 8, 15, 21, 23, 24

For More Information

Gonzalez, Echo Elise. *Biggest, Fastest, Smallest, Slowest!*. Chicago, IL: World Book, Inc., 2018.

Pruetz, J. D. *You Can Be a Primatologist*. Washington, DC: National Geographic, 2020.

Schuh, Mari C. *Sea Dragons*. Mankato, MN: Amicus, Amicus Ink, 2021.

Terp, Gail, *Aye-Ayes*. Mankato, MN: Black Rabbit Books, 2023.